Poetry
in
Crystal

Interpretations in crystal of

thirty-one new poems

by contemporary American poets

POETRY IN CRYSTAL

BY STEUBEN GLASS

FIRST EDITION

© Steuben Glass, A Division of Corning Glass Works, 1963
Library of Congress Catalogue Card Number 63—12592
Printed by The Spiral Press, New York,
with plates by The Meriden Gravure Company.

Contents

FOREWORD
by Cecil Hemley — 7

THE NATURE OF THE COLLECTION
by John Monteith Gates — 9

Harvest Morning
CONRAD AIKEN — 12

This Season
SARA VAN ALSTYNE ALLEN — 14

The Maker
W. H. AUDEN — 16

The Dragon Fly
LOUISE BOGAN — 18

A Maze
WITTER BYNNER — 20

To Build a Fire
MELVILLE CANE — 22

Strong as Death
GUSTAV DAVIDSON — 24

Horn of Flowers
THOMAS HORNSBY FERRIL — 26

Threnos
JEAN GARRIGUE — 28

Off Capri
HORACE GREGORY — 30

Stories
DONALD HALL — 32

Orpheus
CECIL HEMLEY — 34

Voyage to the Island
ROBERT HILLYER — 36

The Certainty
JOHN HOLMES — 38

Birds and Fishes
ROBINSON JEFFERS — 40

The Breathing
  DENISE LEVERTOV   42

To a Giraffe
  MARIANNE MOORE   44

The Aim
  LOUISE TOWNSEND NICHOLL   46

Pacific Beach
  KENNETH REXROTH   48

The Victorians
  THEODORE ROETHKE   50

Aria
  DELMORE SCHWARTZ   52

Tornado Warning
  KARL SHAPIRO   54

Partial Eclipse
  W. D. SNODGRASS   56

Who Hath Seen the Wind?
  A. M. SULLIVAN   58

Trip
  HOLLIS SUMMERS   60

Models of the Universe
  MAY SWENSON   62

Standstill
  JOSEPH TUSIANI   64

April Burial
  MARK VAN DOREN   66

Telos
  JOHN HALL WHEELOCK   68

Leaving
  RICHARD WILBUR   70

Bird Song
  WILLIAM CARLOS WILLIAMS   72

BIOGRAPHICAL SKETCHES
  The Poets   77
  The Artists   84

Foreword

CECIL HEMLEY

President, The Poetry Society of America, 1961–1962

Projects such as Poetry in Crystal have great significance; not only do they promote collaboration between the arts, but they help to restore the artist to the culture to which he belongs. As is well known, the artist has in modern times felt himself more and more alienated from his society. The mass culture of an industrialized world has been at such variance with his ideals that he has isolated himself from the main currents of life. This situation has been disastrous both for the artist and the country. In recent months we have seen the Federal Government interesting itself again in poets, composers, painters, etc. What should have been known all along has at last been grasped; a nation cannot afford to neglect the creators of its values. Poetry in Crystal is a sign that the community is also alert to the prime need of modern society; the search for meaning. Technology can supply some of the things required for the good life, but not the good life itself.

Of course, one project is not sufficient to reverse a hundred and fifty years of suspicion and cleavage. But Poetry in Crystal seems to me a start and a start admirably handled. Steuben Glass has given the poets complete freedom. From the very first moment that Arthur A. Houghton, Jr., Steuben's president, proposed the project, it was made clear to all concerned that no narrow commercial interests were to be allowed to interfere with it. It has been a great pleasure for us of The Poetry Society of America to collaborate with Steuben in this unique undertaking.

7

JOHN MONTEITH GATES

Vice President, Steuben Glass

Steuben Glass is grateful to The Poetry Society of America and to the thirty-one poets represented in this collection for their participation in an experiment—the inspiration of design from poetry.

In the Spring of 1961 the Society, in cooperation with Steuben, invited a number of distinguished American poets to submit new, hitherto-unpublished poems from which our glass designers and artist associates might derive themes for designs in crystal. There were two specifications only: that the poems not concern crystal or glass and that they be no fewer than eight nor more than forty lines in length.

Since the founding of Steuben Glass in 1933, we have sought to develop glassmaking in America as an expression of the arts. In our early years we followed the traditional pattern of embellishing a relatively functional object. A bowl, vase, or plate was decorated by copper wheel engraving with a drawing. For these drawings we turned to artists of reputation throughout the world whose particular styles seemed sympathetic to the medium of crystal. More recently, we have attempted to coordinate the drawing or subject matter intimately with the crystal form. This concept requires the closest collaboration between artist and glass designer. Working together, they create a design which grows from an abstract idea to an integrated whole.

With Poetry in Crystal we embarked on a new experiment in which the artists and designers would draw their inspiration from the vast imagination and beauty of poetry. It was a challenge quite unlike that of our previous collections. Now three forces would be involved: the poet, the artist, and the glass designer. The latter two would attempt to interpret the essence of the poet's expression.

9

Perhaps the greatest challenge here was to try not merely to illustrate the poem but to reveal its spirit, or song, or theme, in a crystal form that would have its own artistic entity. To this end the designers had to make a synthesis, or distillation, of the poetry—susceptible of interpretation. In some cases this interpretation has been literal, in others abstract.

This enterprise was of absorbing interest to our designers. Never before had a project so captured their imagination. As the poems were received, they were re-typed without the name of the poet. When several poems had been assembled, copies of each were given to the artist-designers for their study and selection. Only after a poem had been chosen by an artist or glass designer was the poet's name disclosed.

Obviously, some poems were more difficult of translation than others. Often months elapsed before the artist could visualize a potential interpretation in crystal.

The designs were developed in one of three ways. In some cases, the glass designer first conceived his own interpretation of the poem and then called in an artist who, if sympathetic with the concept, developed the engraving in harmony with the development of the form. In other cases, an artist, having studied the poem, submitted his interpretation for the design of the engraving; the glass designer then evolved a form to complement or supplement the artist's drawing. In yet other cases, our own designers have created the designs in their entirety.

In the last analysis, however, creative forces are dependent on the craftsmen by whose hands the concepts are brought into reality; without the glassworkers' great skills there would be no collection. In addition to offering our thanks to the poets, artists, and designers, we happily offer the glassworkers our admiration for the superb and delicate translation of these poetic themes.

Poetry
in
Crystal

Harvest Morning

Now that body's older
body begs
send the mind to walk
but not the legs.
A mile off still,
we'll see the barley clearly,
and know that this year's harvest
will be early.

CONRAD AIKEN

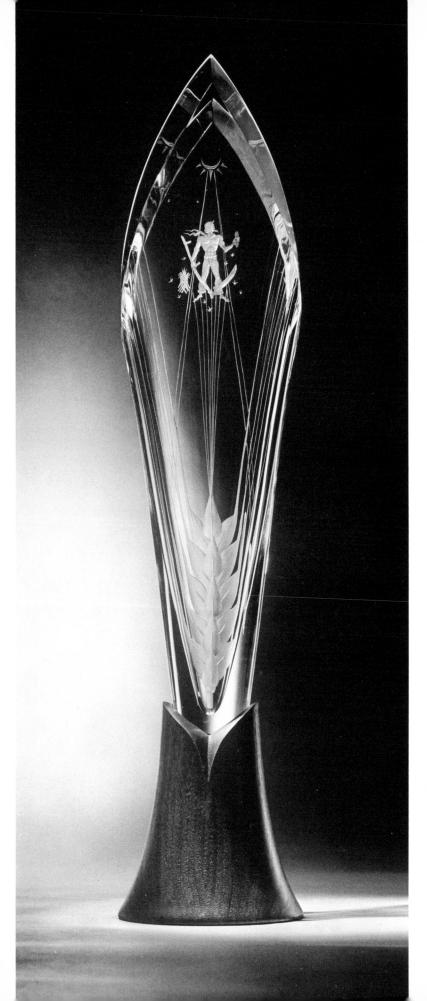

Glass design
by Lloyd Atkins
Engraving design
by Bruce Moore

This Season

So deep a fire does burn, deep, deep within,
Deeper than bones that shape the earthly frame.
Surely such fire must send an emanation
Along the voice and from the wary eyes.

The chin, once vulnerable and round,
Lifted with innocent joy, grows thin and sharp,
Watchful for sorrow's wound. The lips that curved
In trust long hours ago, turn downward now,
Following resignation's flow.
The breasts, once tender and serene,
Apples rounded, hinting of summer,
But still stroked with green,
Are heavy now and weary on the bough.
The body that welcomed assault by a wild sea
And leaned in rapture to the fiercest wind,
Is blurred and slack incredibly.

Incredibly . . . the inmost Self refuses to accept this season.
All the clocks strike the final hour, but there is a climate
Blooming beyond reason, a place where the same morning
Lifts its flower, carrying the leaves of love
In widening eddies to the retreating snows.

SARA VAN ALSTYNE ALLEN

 Glass design by Donald Pollard · Engraving design by Alexander Seidel

The Maker

Unmarried, near-sighted, rather deaf,
This anonymous dwarf,
The legendary ancestor
Of Gunsmiths to His Majesty
And other bespoke houses,
Every museum visitor knows him.

Excluded by his cave
From weather and events, he reckons
Days by the job done and at night
Dreams of the Perfect Object, war to him
A scarcity of bronze, the fall of princes
A change of customer.

Not a musician: songs
Encourage laboring demes, amuse the idle,
But would distract a self-appointed worker
From measuring a hammer's dactyl.
And not an orator: sophists
Don't do metallurgy.

His prices are high and if he doesn't like you
He won't oblige: the Quality
Are made to learn their charm is useless,
A threat fatal. He will deliver
In his good time, not yours: he has no rival
And he knows you know it.

His love, embodied in each useful wonder,
Can't save them in our world from insult
But may avenge it: beware, then, maladroit
Thumb-sucking children of all ages,
Lest on your mangled bodies the court verdict
Be Death by Misadventure.

W. H. AUDEN

 Glass design by Donald Pollard · Engraving design by Sidney Waugh

The
Dragon Fly

You are made of almost nothing
But of enough
To be great eyes
And diaphanous double vans;
To be ceaseless movement,
Unending hunger,
Grappling love.

Link between water and air,
Earth repels you.
Light touches you only to shift into iridescence
Upon your body and wings.

Twice-born, predator,
You split into the heat.
Swift beyond calculation or capture
You dart into the shadow
Which consumes you.

You rocket into the day.
But at last, when the wind flattens the grasses,
For you, the design and purpose stop.

And you fall
With the other husks of summer.

LOUISE BOGAN

 Glass design by George Thompson · Engraving design by Bruce Moore

A Maze

Is a name they call a path
With no easy end
Let it amaze your eye
But not stall your spirit
Be yours the recourse
Of a power
Which when it created a universe
May have left a way out

WITTER BYNNER

 Designed by Lloyd Atkins

To Build
a Fire

The hearth waits,
Clean and bare and ready.

First:
To lay the paper,
A bed of prose to start with.

Then:
Artfully, bit by bit,
Add shavings,
Curling phrases,
Kindling symbols.

Contrive a rhythmic nest of sticks
And crown it with symmetric logs.

Finally:
Loosen and unclog,
That air may flow
And flame may catch.

MELVILLE CANE

 Designed by Lloyd Atkins

Strong
as Death

"For love is strong as death" – SONG OF SOLOMON

Death compassed me with sword and wing
(how lordly was this prince of pride,
this archangelic king!).

"If Love," I said, "is strong as death,
grant me, O prince, a brief reprieve:
once more, in this harsh world of fever and flight,
to wake and sing."

Death sheathed his sword (I thought I heard him sigh).
He spoke (and Love itself drew nigh
to hear the favoring or fateful word).
"I give you leave," he said.

"Then Love," I cried, *"is* strong as death!"

The seraph stirred (his pinions were a throng)
and in the tongue of angels made reply:

"Not Love, but Song."

GUSTAV DAVIDSON

 Glass design by Donald Pollard · Engraving design by Elizabeth Silvagni

Horn of Flowers

Lost in the darkest canyon in the world,
I stuck a staff of lightning into the ground
And let it cool and quiver 'til the sound
Of mountains falling down
Echoed no more
And all was night and blacker than before.

But in that half-forever instant of
The light of lightning shriller than the sun
The jagged canyon changed to a radiant valley
I wandered peacefully
And all alone,
And myth-white, mystical, beyond belief,
My eyes beheld a child, a naked boy
Spiking a hollow horn from a sapphire bull
To the amber gloss of the trunk
Of a lone pine tree.

The luminous boy-child filled the hollow horn
With white white flowers,
The very whitest flowers,
Strange fronds of music interlaced the air,
A golden rose gleamed from three blades of grass
And all the flowers of heaven and earth
Were there.

Who was this boy my ancient eyes beheld?
None but myself could have spiked the horn to the tree,
None but myself could roam these far lost canyons,
None but myself could see what I could see.

I asked myself: "Where did you fare this midnight?"
I answered: "I went wandering with a boy."
"What boy?"
"A sunrise boy I sometimes wander with . . .
I cannot answer you more reasonably."

THOMAS HORNSBY FERRIL

26

 Glass design by Lloyd Atkins · Engraving design by Clare Leighton

Threnos

Our leaves and lakes, our woods,
Those shutters that did bar us from the night
Against which yellowness did fall so dark,
Our leaves have fallen and our lakes dried up.
Fly not, you crows, by echoing woods this way.
The yellow floors of woods receive us not.
The grimy boughs are broke, the nests are down,
And now the gusty halls are walked by wind.
No other tenant's left. Though we have ghosts
We think might walk if grief's a ghost
Although there is no grave to tend
Nor proper way of making epitaph.
How may you dig a grave for poor dead love?
He's but a spectre in the side
And haunted thought. No more than that.

Yet when we spoke our bitter words
I would the leaves had tumbled down
To muffle us and make us sleep
Nor fed by robins nor at all
To wait beneath that kindly pall—
A better way to be with faithless joy
Than this!
To wait until we woke to sober sense—
I rave.
For winter's come with chilling rains to take
The last of leaves and traveling birds away.
And now the sombre pines their needles drop
In early bouts and struggles with the north.
Thy hands are cold to me. Thy lips hear not.

JEAN GARRIGUE

 Designed by Donald Pollard

Off Capri

Beyond the rocks, the beach—
a flash of water:
white foam, and where it turns, the sea-green fires.
Was that a hand,
raised head, and a white shoulder?
Was that a dolphin in the broken wave,
the ancient white, night-rider of the sea,

or deep sea lioness who turns her side
in flaming spray
against the falling sun?
Life within life is there,
and disappears
to deeper reach of seas beneath far waters
to wake, to rise again as fair Dione,
Mother of Venus, earliest of mermaids:

her glittering arms held high,
her white hands braiding
the sea-anemone in green-gold hair,
her eyes the fire of jewels against the sunset—

a careless bathing quean:
men drown with her;
she is no mistress for the wary sailor:
she smiles, he turns,
then feels himself afraid—
only a god could take her in those waters,
herself a goddess for a mortal moment
before the waters close above her head.

HORACE GREGORY

 Glass design by George Thompson · Engraving design by Sidney Waugh

Stories

I look at the rock and the house;
I look at the boat on the river;
I sit on the colored stone
and listen to stories:

the mountain shudders
at the breath of a lizard
and the stream disappears
in a tunnel of jewels;

the walk of a young girl
into darkness and winds
when a snake hisses
with the voice of a cavern;

when the rock turns to air
the sun touches
her body, and diamonds
and the talking lake:

cool air at noon,
light on deep water,
fire at night
in the squares of the winter.

DONALD HALL

 Glass design by George Thompson · Engraving design by Sidney Waugh

Orpheus

I must find her;
Here in some meadow of myself
The song of an imaginary bird
May be her speech,
Or a flower growing in the shade
Of a thought
May have roots that reach
Through the ambiguous shadows
Into the night.
It is my destiny to fracture time
And climb
To silence through the breach,
To touch a memory
And with a word
Kiss it awake.
I sing and as the music
Glistens,
Others see her shape.
I listen but I know
The face is only mist.
The chord I need
Is hidden in my grief.

CECIL HEMLEY

 Glass design by George Thompson · Engraving design by Tom Vincent

Voyage to the Island

A beam wind fills the sails; our wingëd sloop
Over the Caribbean drenched with light
From the full moon flies on, threading a group
Of islands black against the luminous night.

The tiller's pull throbs with a living force
From sea and wind and rudder to command
The boat along her phosphorescent course,
Flinging the pallid fire on either hand.

Astern the wake of braided moonlight streams
Like memory diminishing through time;
Not miles alone but all my long life seems
Left far behind me in another clime.

The overcrowded past and I will be
Ghosts to each other in a little while.
I change our course; the sloop is running free
Among the islands toward the remotest isle.

Yet Love is with me here, my hand on hers—
One reassuring touch and then withdrawn;
And I can steer through coral barriers
More surely for her sake into the dawn,

Which now with sudden radiance brings to view
The palm-green mountains and the turquoise strip
Of water over the white sand, and blue,
Deep sapphire blue, the waves around our ship.

One life is past, another has begun;
We who are old arrive beyond the dark,
Beyond death, and beneath the eternal sun
Drop anchor, furl our sails, and disembark.

ROBERT HILLYER

 Designed by George Thompson

The Certainty

Though I ignore my geological past
As if out of sight is out of mind,
I have remembered the water-table
That under all, not far down, never
To be seen by man, we live or die of.
Three grandparents lived into my time,
My three children will outlast it.
My father died before my first wife,
My mother before my second had our son.
I have buried all the sins, not all
The virtues, bought food, made books.
I have forgotten, I have wasted, I
Survive my sources and my given selves.

The waters of earth rise in the earth.
They seep flatwise between rock-layers,
Leak into closed caves, drench ground,
Meet rivers, tides, and rain sieved down,
And stand agreed at the place and time
For a wetted floor under the carpet
We scrape at, build on, name, and own.
They say there's enough water underground
To cover the world a half mile deep.
Rivers move in that dark. Oceans.
Life of no known shape hangs there.
Wet. Wet. The everlasting slow waters.

I tore a hole twice my height deep
At the foot of the hill back of my house,
And watched the bottom dampen, then fill,
Then stop, and that was the water-table.
Floor. Table. Carpet. What helpless names.
I might as well bite my arm, the blood
Comes from the whole body of the world.
I never lift water to my mouth now
But I bury my face in flood, and drink.

JOHN HOLMES

 Glass design by Donald Pollard· Engraving design by Dale Joe

Birds and Fishes

Every October millions of little fish come along the shore,
Coasting this granite edge of the continent
On their lawful occasions: but what a festival for the
    sea-fowl.
What a witches' sabbath of wings
Hides the dark water. The heavy pelicans shout "Haw!" like
    Job's friend's warhorse
And dive from the high air, the cormorants
Slip their long black bodies under the water and hunt like
    wolves
Through the green half-light. Screaming the gulls watch,
Wild with envy and malice, cursing and snatching. What
    hysterical greed!
What a filling of pouches! the mob-
Hysteria is nearly human—these decent birds!—as if they
    were finding
Gold in the street. It is better than gold,
It can be eaten: and which one in all this fury of wildfowl
    pities the fish?
No one certainly. Justice and mercy
Are human dreams, they do not concern the birds nor the
    fish nor eternal God.
However—look again before you go.
The wings and the wild hungers, the wave-worn skerries,
    the bright quick minnows
Living in terror to die in torment—
Man's fate and theirs—and the island rocks and immense
    ocean beyond, and Lobos
Darkening above the bay: they are beautiful?
That is their quality: not mercy, not mind, not goodness,
    but the beauty of God.

ROBINSON JEFFERS

 Glass design by Donald Pollard · Engraving design by Robert Vickrey

The
Breathing

An absolute
patience.
Trees stand
up to their knees in
fog. The fog
slowly flows
uphill.
       White
cobwebs, the grass
leaning where deer
have looked for apples.
The woods
from brook to where
the top of the hill looks
over the fog, send up
not one bird.
So absolute, it is
no other than
happiness itself, a breathing
too quiet to hear.

DENISE LEVERTOV

 Designed by Don Wier

To a
Giraffe

if it is unpermissible, in fact fatal
to be personal and undesirable

to be literal—detrimental as well
if the eye is not innocent—does it mean that

one can live only on top leaves that are small
reachable only by a beast that is tall?—

of which the giraffe is the best example—
the unconversational animal.

When plagued by the psychological
a creature can be unbearable

that could have been irresistible;
or to be exact exceptional

since less conversational
than some emotionally-tied-in-knots animal.

After all
consolations of the metaphysical
can be profound. In Homer, existence

is flawed; transcendence, conditional;
the journey from sin to redemption, perpetual.*

MARIANNE MOORE

*Ennis Rees summarizes the Odyssey, I feel,
when he finds expressed in it, "the conditional
nature of existence, the consolations of the
metaphysical: the journey from sin to redemption."

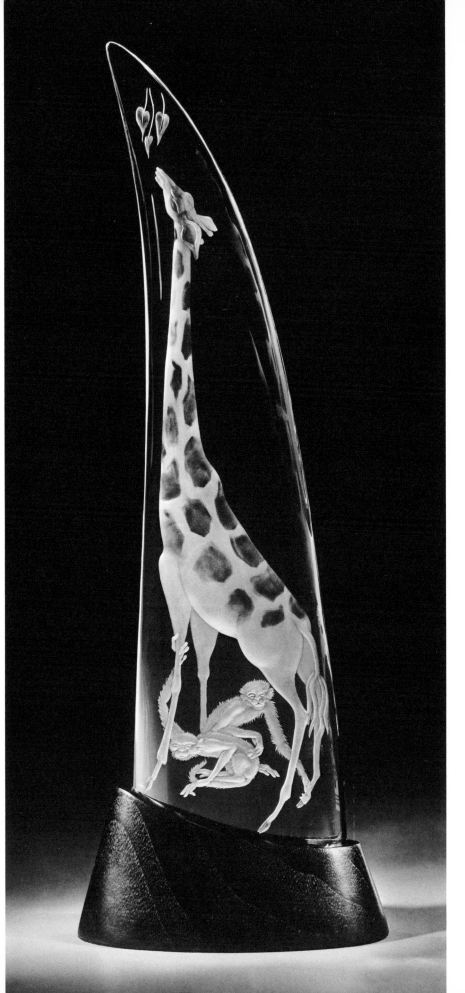

*Glass design
by Lloyd Atkins
Engraving design
by Frank Eliscu*

The Aim

Sun and a bush and a shadow leap toward me
As true as an arrow,
Flung on my sight like a being newborn
Or a sheep of one shear.
Odd, after years I have herded the pasture,
That now of a sudden
The ambient fleece of the world should be shorn
And the creature stand clear,
In this line of the light and the bush and the shadow,
The ultimate arrow.

LOUISE TOWNSEND NICHOLL

 Designed by George Thompson

Pacific Beach

for Phyllis, on her arrival in San Francisco

This is the sea called peaceful,
And tonight it is quiet
As undulant flesh under
The October waning moon.
Late night, not a moving car
On all the moonlit Coast Highway.
No sound but the offshore bells
And the long, recurrent hiss
Of windless surf. "Sophocles
Long ago heard it by the
Aegean." I drive eighty
Miles an hour through the still,
Moonfilled air. The surf withdraws,
Returns, and brings into my
Mind the turgid ebb and flow
Of human loyalty—
The myriad ruined voices
That have said, "Ah, love, let us
Be true to one another."
The moon lured voyagers sleep
In all the voiceless city.
Far out on the horizon
The lights of the albacore
Fleet gleam like a golden town
In another country.

KENNETH REXROTH

for music—the melody of Debussy's posthumous "Trio Sonata"

 Glass design by Donald Pollard · Engraving design by Jacob Landau

The Victorians

O the gondolets, the mandolins, the twangling of the lutes,
The girls all dressed in crinoline among the flowers and fruits—

The flowers all symbolical, the lily and the rose,
And how the sherry blossomed on the end of grandma's nose.

The maiden sighs and turns away; the maiden she relents,
Attracted by the glitter of a pile of five per cents.

They danced beneath the arbors, they strolled upon the grass,
O never aware, O never aware of what would come to pass.

THEODORE ROETHKE

 Glass design by George Thompson · Engraving design by Don Wier

Aria

FROM *Kilroy's Carnival*

" —Kiss me there where pride is glittering
   Kiss me where I am ripened and round fruit
   Kiss me wherever, however I am supple, bare and flare
   (Let the bell be rung as long as I am young:
           let ring and fly like a great bronze wing!)
   Until I am shaken from blossom to root."

" — I'll kiss you wherever you think you are poor,
   Wherever you shudder, feeling striped or barred,
   Because you think you are bloodless, skinny or marred:
           Until, until
         your gaze has been stilled—
   Until you are shamed again no more!
   I'll kiss you until your body and soul
           the mind in the body being fulfilled—
   Suspend their dread and civil war!"

DELMORE SCHWARTZ

 Glass design by Lloyd Atkins · Engraving design by Leon Kroll

Tornado Warning

It is a beauteous morning but the air turns sick,
The April freshness seems to rot, a curious smell.
Above the wool-pack clouds a rumor stains the sky,
A fallow color deadening atmosphere and mind.
The air gasps horribly for breath, sucking itself
In spasms of sharp pain, light drifts away.
Women walk on grass, a few husbands come home,
Bushes and trees stop dead, children gesticulate,
Radios warn to open windows, tell where to hide.

The pocky cloud mammato-cumulus comes on,
Downward-projecting bosses of brown cloud grow
Lumps on lymphatic sky, blains, tumors, and dugs,
Heavy cloud-boils that writhe in general disease of sky,
While bits of hail clip at the crocuses and clunk
At cars and windowglass.

                      We cannot see the mouth,
We cannot see the mammoth's neck hanging from cloud,
Snout open, lumbering down ancient Nebraska
Where dinosaur lay down in deeps of clay and died,
And towering elephant fell and billion buffalo.
We cannot see the horror-movie of the funnel-cloud
Snuffing up cows, crazing the cringing villages,
Exploding homes and barns, bursting the level lakes.

KARL SHAPIRO

 Glass design by Lloyd Atkins · Engraving design by Bruce Moore

Partial Eclipse

Last night's eclipse, 99 percent complete,
seemed at times to be total because
of light mists and low-hanging clouds.

—RADIO NEWS REPORT

Once we'd packed up your clothes
    It was something to talk about:
The full moon, how it rose
    Red, went pale, and went out

As that slow shadow crossed—
    The way Time might erase
Its blackboard: one cheek lost,
    The eyes, most of the face

Hovering dim as a ghost,
    As the dark print of some light
That seared the eyes, almost,
    Lives on in the lids, clenched tight.

Yet still one brilliant sliver
    Stayed, thin as a fingernail;
Then that went vague, would shiver,
    Till even it would fail

And the sky blank, bereft.
    But no; the mists drifted on;
Something, something was left.
    Next morning you had gone.

W. D. SNODGRASS

 Designed by James Houston

Who Hath Seen the Wind?

You who are stalking the wind shall follow
    her only by symbols.

Curled in a cloud, a tiger is sleeping,
    her tail a zephyr caressing the sun.

Waking, she mews by chimney pots, or strums
    stiff reeds in the marshes

But when lightning splinters the sky, and
    echoes of anvils pummel the thirsty arroyos

She wears black capes of a witch, and spins
    tiptoe on livid horizons,

Lifting up trees by their hair, and sucking out
    walls of the farmhouse:

Tormentor of birches, assassin of oaks, vandal
    who tilts the cap of the silo,

Etcher of prisms caught in spume-tossed
    nets of the tidal moment,

Ghost in the grass, rippler of wheat with the
    touch of her garments,

Mocker of gargoyles, weaver of mischief when
    the weathervane glints in the starlight,

Mourner of yesterdays in memory's deep shadows,
    grieving by moats and by cloisters,

Invisible always, and naked never, but
    clothed by the necromancers

The proof of the wind is the shape and the sound
    and no man has ever unmasked her.

A. M. SULLIVAN

 Designed by Donald Pollard

Trip

We drove a little way out of town
To watch some children wander
Barefooted up and down
A silvergreen pond

Surrounded by some hickory trees
That bore blue lilies
Under a sky friezed
With calligraphy.

We could not possibly imagine
The lilies, or the children,
Or what the letters meant.
And we turned around again.

HOLLIS SUMMERS

 Glass design by George Thompson · Engraving design by Robert Vickrey

Models
of the
Universe

1.

At moment X
the universe began.
It began at point X.
Since then,
through the Hole in a Nozzle,
stars have spewed. An
inexhaustible gush
populates the void forever.

2.

The universe was there
before time ran.
A grain
slipped in the glass:
the past began.
The Container
of the Stars expands;
the sand
of matter multiplies forever.

3.

From zero radius
to a certain span,
the universe, a Large Lung
specked with stars,
inhales time
until, turgent, it can
hold no more,
and collapses. Then
space breathes, and inhales again,
and breathes again: Forever.

MAY SWENSON

 Glass design by Donald Pollard · Engraving design by William Philips

Standstill

Something is standing still
around or in me,
something that is or could be
the world with its last heaven
or even the end of my will
or my soul.

For the first time, if ever at all,
my mind now follows my body asleep
and knows the name
of the water deep
now that all water is still
and seems no more to be water
just as my will unafraid of tears
is not my will — is not my birth.

And I can see the worth
of things, the size
and purpose of each star
and of man's earth
in the skies,
and my own will
a useful, useless speck apart
and very far.

I cannot tell
what all this is
and what I am —
heartbeat or sham,
life of another or will
of my own.
Something, I feel, if not lost yet,
is standing still.

JOSEPH TUSIANI

 Designed by George Thompson

April
Burial

On this chill day
Let earth be warm,
Receiving the child,
Undoing the harm.

Death was by day.
Then let no light
Enter this grave,
This natural night.

Beneath all days
Leave these together:
Earth and the quick girl,
Quiet forever.

MARK VAN DOREN

*Glass design
by Lloyd Atkins
Engraving design
by Leon Kroll*

Telos

Give me your hand
By these grey waters—
The day is ending.

Already the first
Faint star pierces
The veil of heaven.

Oh, the long way
We two have come,
In joy, together,

To these grey shores
And quiet waters
And the day's ending!

The day is ending.
The journey is ended.
Give me your hand.

JOHN HALL WHEELOCK

 Designed by Don Wier

Leaving

As we left the garden-party
By the far gate,
There were many loitering on
Who had come late

And a few arriving still,
Though the lawn lay
Like a fast-draining shoal
Of ochre day.

Curt shadows in the grass
Hatched every blade,
And now on pediments
Of mounting shade

Stood all our friends — iconic,
Now, in mien,
Half lost in dignities
Till now unseen.

There were the hostess' hands
Held out to greet
The scholar's limp, his wife's
Quick-pecking feet,

And there was wit's cocked head,
And there the sleek
And gaze-enameled look
Of beauty's cheek.

We saw now, loitering there
Knee-deep in night,
How even the wheeling children
Moved in a rite

Or masque, or long charade
Where we, like these,
Had blundered into grand
Identities,

Filling our selves as sculpture
Fills the stone!
We had not played so well,
If we had known.

RICHARD WILBUR

 Glass design by Donald Pollard · Engraving design by Frank Eliscu

Bird Song

It is May on every hand
when the Towhee sings
to his silent mate

at the bottom of
the garden
flaunting his startling

colors moving restlessly
from one
leafless magnolia twig

to another—
announcing spring is
here spring is here

WILLIAM CARLOS WILLIAMS

 Glass design by George Thompson · Engraving design by Alexander Seidel

Biographical
Sketches

THE POETS

CONRAD AIKEN was born in Savannah, Georgia, attended Harvard University, and now lives on Cape Cod with his wife Mary Hoover, the painter. Among his more than twenty-five published volumes of poetry are *Preludes for Memnon* (1931), *Landscape West of Eden* (1933), *Time in the Rock* (1936), *Brownstone Eclogues* (1942), and more recently, *Collected Poems* (1953), *Sheepfold Hill* (1957), and *Selected Poems* (1961). He has also published collections of short stories, the latest being *The Short Stories of Conrad Aiken*; novels, such as *Blue Voyage*; criticism, as in *A Reviewer's ABC*; a play *Mr. Arcularis*; and an autobiography, *Ushant: An Essay*. He held the Chair of Poetry at the Library of Congress for two years, and has received the Pulitzer Prize, the Bollingen Prize, and the National Book Award, as well as many other honors.

SARA VAN ALSTYNE ALLEN attended Pomona College, receiving a Bachelor's degree in 1927. She has contributed poems to *Harper's Magazine*, *Saturday Review*, *The American Scholar*, *Poetry* magazine, *The New Yorker*, *The Nation*, *Yale Review*, and other magazines, and has appeared in numerous poetry anthologies, including the *Thomas Mount Anthology*. In 1952 she won the second prize in the annual awards of The Poetry Society of America. She is a member of Phi Beta Kappa, the Pen and Brush, the Craftsman Group, and was for a number of years on the executive board of The Poetry Society of America.

W. H. AUDEN was born in England and attended Oxford University. He came to the United States in 1939, subsequently becoming an American citizen. Author of many books of verse, plays, and criticism, he published his *Selected Poems* in 1938, his *Collected Poetry* in 1945, and his *Collected Shorter Poems 1930–44* in 1950. In 1947 a long poem, *The Age of Anxiety: A Baroque Eclogue*, appeared. With Chester Kallman, he wrote the libretto for Stravinsky's opera, *The Rake's Progress*. His plays, *The Dog Beneath the Skin* and *The Ascent of F. 6*, written with Christopher Isherwood, have been frequently performed. Among his awards for poetry are a Guggenheim Fellowship in 1942, the Bollingen Prize in 1953, and the National Book Award in 1956. He has edited a number of anthologies of poetry.

LOUISE BOGAN was born in Maine, and attended Boston University. Her books of poems include *Body of This Death* (1923), *Dark Summer* (1929), *The Sleeping Fury* (1937), *Poems and New Poems* (1941), and *Collected Poems, 1923–53* (1954); her books of criticism are *Achievement in American Poetry, 1900–1950* (1951) and *Selected Criticism* (1955). She has contributed verse, criticism, and fiction to *The New Yorker*, *The Nation*, *New Republic*, and *Poetry: A Magazine of Verse*. In 1944 she was a fellow in American Letters at the Library of Congress and in 1945–46 held the Chair of Poetry there. Among her awards are the John Reed Memorial Prize from *Poetry* magazine, two Guggenheim Fellowships, the Harriet Monroe Poetry Award given by the University of Chicago, a grant from the National Institute of Arts & Letters, the Bollingen Prize, and the Senior Creative Arts Award in poetry from Brandeis University.

WITTER BYNNER was graduated from Harvard in 1902, having been on the staff of the *Harvard Advocate*. He traveled extensively in the Orient, particularly in China; and Chinese poetry has influenced his own. Since 1922, he has lived in Santa Fe, New Mexico, and Chapala, Jalisco, Mexico. The author of some thirty books, he brought out his first volume of verse, *Young Harvard*, in 1907. Among his many titles are: *The Way of Life According to Laotzu* (1944), a transliteration; *Take Away the Darkness* (1947), verse; *Journey with Genius* (1951), a prose portrait of D. H. and Frieda Lawrence; *A Book of Lyrics* (1955); and *New Poems 1960*. He is a collector and donor of Chinese paintings and jades, Mexican, Southwestern, and Indian artifacts. From 1920 to 1922, he was president of The Poetry Society of America and has been since 1946 a chancellor in the Academy of American Poets.

MELVILLE CANE, born in Plattsburg, New York, received his B.A. at Columbia University and his LL.B. from its law school. He joined the firm of Ernst, Lowenstein & Cane in 1905, and is senior member of the present firm of Ernst, Cane, Berner & Gitlin. In 1919 he organized the publishing house of Harcourt, Brace and Howe, now Harcourt, Brace & World, Inc., of which he is a director and counsel. He specializes in copyright law and allied fields. Among his published works are *A Wider Arc* (1947), *And Pastures New* (1956), *Bullet-Hunting* (1960), all books of poetry, and *Making A Poem*, a prose work published in 1953 and reissued in 1962 as a paperback. In 1948 he was awarded the Columbia University Medal for excellence in law and poetry. He was coeditor of *The Man From Main Street: A Sinclair Lewis Reader* (1953), and of *The Golden Year* (1960), an anthology of poems by members of The Poetry Society of America.

GUSTAV DAVIDSON is executive secretary and fellow of The Poetry Society of America. He has published books in drama, bibliography, poetry, and angelology. Since 1940 he has directed The Fine Editions Press. His literary prizes include the Lola Ridge Memorial Award, the Lyric Award ($1,000), and the Alexander Droutzkoy Gold Medal for Distinguished Achievement. He is the compiler of *In Fealty to Apollo* (1950), an illustrated history of The Poetry Society, and is senior United States editor of the *Dictionary of International Biography* (1963). He is also a member of the Advisory Committee on the Arts, National Cultural Center. During the summer of 1962 he served as Poet-in-Residence at the Blaffer Trust Foundation in New Harmony, Indiana. Educated at Columbia University, he received there his Bachelor's and Master's degrees.

THOMAS HORNSBY FERRIL entered newspaper work in Denver after serving as a second lieutenant in World War I. His earliest poems were newspaper verses, some of which appeared in his first book, *High Passage* (1926). Later books of poems include *Trial by Time* (1944) and *New and Selected Poems* (1952). He has written plays, one of them—*And Perhaps Happiness* (1957)—winning a prize of $10,000. Besides honorary degrees from universities, he has received many awards, among them *The Nation's* poetry prize, the Oscar Blumenthal Prize from *Poetry* magazine, a Doubleday-Doran prize, a *Forum* award, an award by the Academy of American Poets, and the Robert Frost Poetry Award. Since 1926 he has worked for the Great Western Sugar Company in Denver, editing their magazines, writing books, and making motion pictures on agronomy, animal husbandry, and the handling of farm equipment. He and his wife Helen publish Colorado's oldest weekly newspaper, *The Rocky Mountain Herald*.

JEAN GARRIGUE was born in Indiana. Since 1940 she has lived principally in New York City and on occasion in France and Italy. She attended the University of Chicago and the University of Iowa, and has taught English at Bard College, Queens College, the New School for Social Research, and the University of Connecticut. Her poetry first appeared in "Nine Younger Poets" in *The Kenyon Review* (1941). A larger selection, "Thirty-six Poems and a Few Songs," was included in *Five Young American Poets* (1944). Miss Garrigue has published three additional volumes of poetry, the most recent being *A Water Walk by Villa d'Este*, which appeared in both England and the United States in 1959. Among her honors are an award from the National Institute of Arts & Letters and fellowships from the Rockefeller and Guggenheim Foundations.

HORACE GREGORY, born in Milwaukee, studied at the University of Wisconsin, receiving a Bachelor's degree in 1923. A free-lance writer until 1934, he contributed to *The Nation*, *The Atlantic Monthly*, *New Republic*, and other magazines. His first book of poems was *Chelsea Rooming House*, published in 1930. His *Selected Poems* appeared in 1951, and his most recent volume is *Medusa in Gramercy Park* (1961). He has also published criticism, such as *The Dying Gladiators and Other Essays* (1961); biographical works on D. H. Lawrence and Amy Lowell; and has edited an anthology of religious verse. He has received the Lyric and Levinson prizes from *Poetry* magazine, the Loines Award, a Guggenheim Fellowship, and the Academy of American Poets Award for "distinguished contribution to American poetry."

DONALD HALL, born in New Haven, Connecticut, attended Harvard University, Oxford University, and Stanford University. From 1954 to 1957 he was a junior fellow of the Society of Fellows at Harvard. He is now an associate professor of English at the University of Michigan, where he has taught since 1957. His first book of poems, *Exiles and Marriages*, was a Lamont Poetry Selection and appeared in 1955. His second book of poetry was *The Dark Houses* (1958). In 1961 his prose memoir, *String Too Short to be Saved*, was published. While at Oxford he received the Newdigate Prize. He was poetry editor of *The Paris Review* 1953–1961.

CECIL HEMLEY was born in New York City, received a Bachelor's degree at Amherst College in 1934 and a Master's degree at the University of Chicago in 1950. From 1942 to 1946 he served in World War II as a first lieutenant in the United States Army. He is now editor-in-chief of Noonday Press, which he founded in 1951; he is also an editor at Farrar, Straus and Cudahy, publishers. His books include several volumes of poetry, *Porphyry's Journey*, published in 1951, *Twenty Poems* (1956), and *In the Midnight Wood* (1960), as well as two novels, *The Experience* (1960) and *Young Crankshaw* (1963). He was codirector of *Noonday Review* from 1958 to 1960, and president of The Poetry Society of America in 1961 and 1962.

ROBERT HILLYER (1895–1961). A graduate of Harvard University, Robert Hillyer served for many years on its faculty; in 1937 he was named Boylston Professor of Rhetoric and Oratory. In 1949 and again from 1951 to 1953 he was president of The Poetry Society of America. His published work includes more than sixteen volumes of poetry. His first book was *Sonnets and Other Lyrics* (1917); more recent books were *The Suburb by the Sea* (1952), a collection of satirical lyrics, *The Relic and Other Poems* (1957), and *Collected Poems* (1961). He also wrote novels and literary criticism. Among his awards were the Garrison Prize, won in 1916, and the Pulitzer Prize, won in 1934 for his volume *Collected Verse*, which had been published in 1933. In 1944 he resigned from the faculty of Harvard to devote himself primarily to writing.

JOHN HOLMES (1904–1962). Professor of English at Tufts University, John Holmes lived in Medford, Massachusetts, and was regional vice president of The Poetry Society of America. He was graduated from Tufts, attended Harvard University, then taught for two years at Lafayette College before returning to his alma mater, where he taught for twenty-eight years. His several books of poetry include *Map of My Country* (1943) and *The Fortune Teller* (1961). He edited *A Little Treasury of Love Poems* (1950) and *A Complete College Reader*. From 1947 to 1952 he directed the Chautauqua Writers Workshop, and from 1952 until his death, the Tufts Workshop in Poetry. He was Phi Beta Kappa poet at Tufts, Brown University, William and Mary College, and Harvard University, and was a member of the American Academy of Arts & Sciences.

ROBINSON JEFFERS (1887–1962). Son of a Pittsburgh physician, Robinson Jeffers was educated in Europe, at the University of Pittsburgh, and at Occidental College, Los Angeles, where he received his B.A. degree. There followed graduate work in English and study of medicine and forestry. In 1914 a legacy enabled him to buy property in Carmel, California. There he built with his own hands a stone house in which he lived and devoted his life to writing poetry. Among his more than twenty books are *Roan Stallion, Tamar and Other Poems* (1925), *Give Your Heart to the Hawks* (1933), and *Hungerfield* (1954). He wrote four verse plays including *Medea*, a free adaptation from Euripides, which was presented on Broadway with Judith Anderson in the title role. Last of his many honors was the 1960 Shelley Memorial Award from The Poetry Society of America.

DENISE LEVERTOV was born in London, came to the United States in 1948 with her American husband, the novelist Mitchell Goodman, and is now a naturalized citizen. She has one son, Nikolai. During World War II she was a nurse in London hospitals. Her first book of poems was *The Double Image*, published in 1948. Her latest collection is *The Jacob's Ladder* (1961). Her other volumes of verse are *Here & Now* (1957), *Overland to the Islands* (1958), and *With Eyes at the Back of Our Heads* (1959). Among her awards are the Bessie Hokin Prize, a Longview Award, and a Guggenheim Fellowship. She has given readings at many colleges throughout the United States. In 1961 she served as poetry editor of *The Nation*.

MARIANNE MOORE's first book of poetry, *Poems*, was published in 1921 by her friend Bryher—i.e., Winifred Ellerman. Her *Collected Poems* appeared in 1951 and within a year had won the Bollingen Prize, the National Book Award, and the Pulitzer Prize. More recently, in 1961, *A Marianne Moore Reader* appeared, including her prose as well as her verse. The recipient of many honorary degrees, she has also been given the Gold Medal for Poetry by the National Institute of Arts & Letters, the Harriet Monroe Poetry Award from the University of Chicago, the Contemporary Poetry's Patrons' Prize, and a Guggenheim Fellowship. From 1926 to 1929 she was acting editor of the literary magazine, *The Dial*. She now lives in Brooklyn, New York.

LOUISE TOWNSEND NICHOLL is the author of seven books of poetry, the latest of which, *The World's One Clock*, appeared in 1959. Her first book of poems was *Water and Light* (1939). In 1953, *Collected Poems* was published. She was graduated from Smith College, did newspaper work, and then joined the publishing firm of E. P. Dutton & Company, where she was an associate editor for some years. She now maintains her own free-lance editorial office. In 1954 she was awarded a fellowship from the Academy of American Poets, and in 1960 was created a fellow of The Poetry Society of America. She is a member of P.E.N. and of The Catholic Poetry Society of America; and a vice president of The Poetry Society of America.

KENNETH REXROTH, poet, translator, critic, and painter, has lived in San Francisco since 1927. *In What Hour* was his first book of poems, published in 1940; his most recent is *In Defense of the Earth* (1956). Several volumes of his translations have appeared: from the Japanese, Chinese, Spanish, Greek, and Latin. There have also been books of criticism, *The Bird in the Bush* (1959), *Assays* (1962), and literary essays. One of the first abstract painters in the United States, he has had one-man shows in Los Angeles, Santa Monica, New York City, and San Francisco. In 1948 he received a Guggenheim Fellowship, in 1958 an Amy Lowell Fellowship, and he has won a number of awards for his poems. A skier and mountain climber, he does much of his creative writing in the mountains.

THEODORE ROETHKE has said that it took him "ten years to complete one little book" —his first, *Open House* (1941). Since then, he has published four more books of poetry, his 1953 volume, *The Waking: Poems 1933–53*, having been awarded the Pulitzer Prize. In 1958 he was given the Bollingen Prize, in 1959 the Edna St. Vincent Millay Award and the National Book Award, in 1961 the Shelley Memorial Award. His latest book is *"I Am!" Says the Lamb*, published in 1961. He attended the University of Michigan and Harvard University, and was a member of Phi Beta Kappa. He has taught at Lafayette College, Pennsylvania State University, and Bennington College, and is now professor of English and Poet-in-Residence at the University of Washington. One of his great interests is in the oral presentation of poetry.

DELMORE SCHWARTZ, poet, playwright, short story writer, and literary critic, was born in Brooklyn, New York, and attended the universities of Columbia, Wisconsin, New York, and Harvard. He then taught English at Harvard from 1940 to 1947. From 1943 to 1955 he was associated with the literary magazine *Partisan Review*, chiefly as associate editor. His first book of poetry came out in 1938, *In Dreams Begin Responsibilities*; his most recent book of poems, *Summer Knowledge: New and Selected Poems, 1938–58*, was published in 1959 and won the Bollingen Prize. In the same year he was awarded the Shelley Memorial Award. He was a Guggenheim Fellow in 1940, a *Kenyon Review* Fellow in 1957, and has received awards from *Poetry* magazine and the National Institute of Arts & Letters.

KARL SHAPIRO, born in Baltimore, attended the universities of Virginia and Johns Hopkins. His early literary career was spent overseas in Australia, New Guinea, and the surrounding islands, during World War II. *Person, Place and Thing* (1942) and *V-Letter and Other Poems* (1944) were books published during this period. The latter won the Pulitzer Prize in 1945. Many books of verse have followed, among them *Essay on Rime* (1945), *Poems 1942–53* (1953), and *Poems of a Jew* (1958). Critical works have appeared, the most recent being *In Defense of Ignorance* (1960). From 1950 to 1956 he edited *Poetry: A Magazine of Verse*, and since 1956 has edited *Prairie Schooner*, a literary journal. He teaches at the University of Nebraska. In 1947 he was consultant in poetry to the Library of Congress.

W. D. SNODGRASS's first book, *Heart's Needle*, which appeared in 1959, won the Pulitzer Prize for poetry in 1960. Among his other honors are the Ingram-Merrill Award, a *Hudson Review* Fellowship, a Longview Award, a special citation from The Poetry Society of America, and a grant from the National Institute of Arts & Letters. He studied for two years at Geneva College, and then went on to the State University of Iowa where he took a Bachelor's degree in 1949, a Master's degree in 1951, and a Master of Fine Arts degree in 1953. He has taught at Cornell University, at the University of Rochester, and since 1959 at Wayne State University where he is associate professor of English. He contributes essays, poems, and translations to literary magazines.

A. M. SULLIVAN, president of The Poetry Society of America from 1940 to 1943 and from 1950 to 1952, is the author of a number of books. Among the recent titles are *Incident in Silver* (1950), *Psalms of the Prodigal* (1953), and *The Three-Dimensional Man*, a book of essays (1956). He founded the "New Poetry Hour," a radio forum for poets over station WOR and the Mutual Network. Since 1934 he has been in charge of advertising and public relations for Dun & Bradstreet, Inc., and since 1936 an editor of *Dun's Review and Modern Industry*. His honors include medals for his poetry from The Poetry Society of America in 1952 and from The Catholic Poetry Society of America in 1958. He is currently president of The Catholic Poetry Society. He is historiographer and director of the American Irish Historical Society.

HOLLIS SUMMERS, born in Kentucky, attended Georgetown College and the State University of Iowa. He then taught at Georgetown College, going on to the University of Kentucky where he was in 1959 elected Distinguished Professor of the Year by the College of Arts and Sciences. At present he is professor of English at Ohio University. He has published two books of poems, *The Walks Near Athens* (1959) and *Someone Else* (1962), poems for children. Three novels have appeared; the most recent is *The Weather of February* (1957). He has also contributed poems and short stories to many magazines. In 1951 he received a Ford grant to study writing programs in American colleges and universities. The *Saturday Review* Poetry Award was given him in 1957.

MAY SWENSON was born in Logan, Utah, and was graduated from Utah State University. She has contributed poems to *The Nation, Saturday Review, The New Yorker,* and many other magazines. *Another Animal: Poems* (1954) was her first collection. This was followed by *A Cage of Spines* (1958). Her newest book, *To Mix with Time,* will be published in the spring of 1963. Her poems appear in ten anthologies— three of them issued in England, Italy, and Germany. Those published in the United States include *A Treasury of Great American Poetry* (1955), *New Poets No. 2* (1957), *New Poets of England and America* (1957), and *Modern Love Poems* (1961). Among her many awards are a Rockefeller grant, a Guggenheim Fellowship, a Longview Award, and an award from the National Institute of Arts & Letters.

JOSEPH TUSIANI, born in Italy, was graduated from the University of Naples and came to the United States in 1947. He became a citizen in 1956. Chairman of the Italian department of the College of Mount St. Vincent in New York, he also lectures at Hunter College and teaches at New York University. He is director of The Catholic Poetry Society of America and vice president of The Poetry Society of America. The author of many books of poetry and criticism in Italian, including *Sonettisti Americani* (1954) and *Odi Sacre* (1958), he has also published several books in English: *Two Critical Essays on Emily Dickinson* (1952); *The Complete Poems of Michelangelo,* a translation (1960); *Rind and All,* a collection of poems (1962). Scheduled for publication in 1963 is *Lust and Liberty,* a translation of the poems of Machiavelli. In 1956 he was awarded the Greenwood Prize by the Poetry Society, London.

MARK VAN DOREN, though known chiefly as a poet, has published fiction, literary criticism, biography, and a play about Abraham Lincoln. His first book of poems was *Spring Thunder and Other Poems* (1924) and his most recent was *Morning Worship and Other Poems* (1960). Over

a dozen volumes of verse appeared between these dates, his *Collected Poems* (1939) receiving the Pulitzer Prize. *Selected Poems* came out in 1954. Among his prose works are *Home with Hazel and Other Stories* (1957) and *The Autobiography of Mark Van Doren* (1958). After graduating from the University of Illinois and Columbia University, he taught English at Columbia from 1920 to 1959, retiring at that time to his home in Connecticut where, for years, he had done most of his writing on summer vacations and during sabbaticals.

JOHN HALL WHEELOCK, born in Far Rockaway, Long Island, attended Harvard University, where he edited the *Harvard Monthly* and was Class Poet (1908). He then studied at universities in Germany, writing a great deal of verse during this period. In 1910 he returned to America, shortly thereafter becoming associated with Charles Scribner's Sons; he became an editor in 1926. His early poems, he has said, were strongly influenced by Shelley and Swinburne. *The Human Fantasy* (1911) was his first book of poems. Among the many which followed, *Collected Poems* (1936) was awarded the Golden Rose by the New England Poetry Society, and *Poems Old and New* (1956) received the Borestone Mountain Poetry Award and the Ridgely Torrence Memorial Award. His *The Gardener and Other Poems* (1961) was co-winner of the Bollingen Prize in Poetry for that year.

RICHARD WILBUR attended Amherst College, where he edited the college newspaper, anticipating a career in journalism. Not until World War II took him to Cassino, Anzio, and the Siegfried Line did he begin seriously to write poetry. After the war he attended Harvard and became a member of the Society of Fellows there from 1947 to 1950 and a member of the English department from 1950 to 1954. His first book of poems, *The Beautiful Changes,* appeared in 1947, followed by *Ceremony, and Other Poems* (1950), *A Bestiary,* an anthology (1955), *Molière's Misanthrope,* a translation (1955), *Things of This World* (1956), *Poems 1943–56* (1957), *Candide,* a comic opera, with Lillian Hellman (1957), and *Advice to a Prophet* (1961). His awards include the Harriet Monroe and Oscar Blumenthal Prizes, the Prix de Rome, the National Book Award, the Pulitzer Prize, and Guggenheim and Ford Fellowships. Since 1957 he has been professor of English at Wesleyan University.

WILLIAM CARLOS WILLIAMS, poet, playwright, novelist, and physician, was born in Rutherford, New Jersey, where he still lives and where for many years he practiced medicine. He has written and published a great number of books of poetry and prose. His first volume was *Poems* (1909). Between 1946 and 1951 there appeared the four books comprising his major poetic work, *Paterson*, the story of an industrial city on the Passaic River. *Selected Poems* came out in 1949, and his *Autobiography of William Carlos Williams* in 1951. His play *Many Loves* became part of the permanent repertory of the Living Theatre in New York. In addition to his honorary degrees from universities, he has won the *Dial* Award, *Poetry*'s Guarantor's Prize, the Loines Award of the National Institute of Arts & Letters, the National Book Award, the Brandeis Award, the Bollingen Prize, and the Academy of American Poets Award.

THE ARTISTS

LLOYD ATKINS, designer, was born in Brooklyn, New York, and entered Pratt Institute in 1941. The following year he joined the United States Army Air Force. After World War II he returned to Pratt, from which he was graduated with a Certificate of Industrial Design. In 1948 he became a member of the Steuben Glass design department, continuing his studies at night to earn a B.I.D. degree from Pratt. His work in crystal has been shown in many Steuben exhibitions, including those at the Palais du Louvre, Paris; Park Lane House, London; the National Gallery of Art, Washington, D.C.; and the Metropolitan Museum of Art, New York.

FRANK ELISCU, sculptor, studied in New York at the Beaux Arts Institute of Design, Pratt Institute, and the Clay Club. A fellow of the National Sculpture Society and associate of the National Academy of Design, he has received several awards for sculpture. His works in bronze and slate have been exhibited by the Pennsylvania Academy of the Fine Arts, Detroit Institute of Arts, Cleveland Museum of Art, and other museums. Among his commissions are a fountain at Brookgreen Gardens, South Carolina; "Atoms for Peace," Ventura, California; and heroic slate horses for the Bankers Trust Building, New York City. His book *Sculpture: Techniques in Clay, Wax and Slate* was published in 1959.

JAMES HOUSTON, graphic artist, painter, and illustrator, was born in Toronto, Canada. He studied at the Toronto Art Gallery, Ontario College of Art, École Grande Chaumière and Atelier 17 in Paris, and with Un-ichi Hiratsuka in Tokyo. For twelve years he was a civil administrator for the Canadian Government in the Eastern Arctic where he fostered the skills of Eskimo carvers and printmakers, assisting with exhibitions of their work throughout the world. In 1962 he joined the design staff of Steuben Glass. Among his works are "The Arctic Color Series," "Exploration," a Quebec mural, and four illustrated books: *Shoot to Live* (1944), *Canadian Eskimo Art* (1954), *Nuki* (1955), and *Iyorama* (1956).

DALE JOE, painter, was born in California, was graduated from the University of California in 1951, and then studied at the California College of Arts and Crafts and other art schools. In 1951 he held his first one-man shows in Santa Barbara and San Francisco and was awarded two first prizes at the San Francisco Museum of Art Annual. There followed other honors, including John Hay Whitney and Fulbright Awards. His work is represented in the San Francisco Museum of Art and in private collections in the United States and Europe. It has been included in exhibitions at the Whitney Museum, Chicago Art Institute, and Smithsonian Institution.

LEON KROLL, painter and lithographer, is a native of New York City, where he studied at the Art Students League and National Academy of Design. He is a member of the American Academy of Arts and Letters, chevalier of the French Legion of Honor, and academician of the National Academy of Design. His paintings are represented in the collections of the principal museums in the United States and have been included in many national and international exhibitions. Among his works are murals in the Justice

Building, Washington, D.C., and in the Senate Chamber, Indianapolis, and the mosaic dome, United States Military Cemetery, Omaha Beach, France.

JACOB LANDAU, painter, lithographer, and engraver, was born in Philadelphia. A graduate of the Philadelphia Museum School of Art, he later studied in Paris and at the New School for Social Research, New York. He has taught at the Philadelphia Museum School of Art and at Pratt Institute. His work has been exhibited in Paris at the Salon d'Automne, Musée de l'Art Moderne, and Galerie Lebar, as well as in museums and galleries in this country, including the Museum of Modern Art, New York, and the Philadelphia Art Alliance. He has illustrated two books: *The Gold Bug and Other Tales* (1953) and *Little Lower Than the Angels* (1955).

CLARE LEIGHTON, printmaker and designer, studied at the Slade School of Art and the County Council Central School of Art in her native London. She came to the United States in 1939, and subsequently became an American citizen. Her prints are included in the permanent collections of the Metropolitan Museum of Art, New York, the Victoria and Albert Museum, London, and other museums in Europe and the United States. She has written and illustrated twelve books, including *Country Matters* (1937) and *Southern Harvest* (1942), and has illustrated many books by other authors. Recently she designed the stained glass windows for St. Paul's Cathedral, Worcester, Massachusetts.

BRUCE MOORE, sculptor, was born in Kansas. He studied at the Pennsylvania Academy of the Fine Arts, spent two summers abroad as winner of the Cresson European Traveling Scholarships, then worked as studio assistant to James Earle Fraser. His animal figures in stone, bronze, clay, and terra cotta are found in the Whitney Museum, the Wichita Art Museum, the Pennsylvania Academy of the Fine Arts, and other collections. Among his recent commissions are sculpture for the National Memorial of the Pacific, Honolulu, and bronze doors for Grace Episcopal Cathedral, San Francisco. During the past fifteen years he has designed more than thirty engraved pieces for Steuben Glass.

WILLIAM PHILIPS, sculptor, studied at Massachusetts Institute of Technology School of Architecture and at Maryland Institute's Rinehart School of Sculpture, graduating with a B.F.A. A member of the National Sculpture Society, he received the Society's John Gregory Award in 1959. His work has been exhibited in New York by the National Sculpture Society and the National Academy of Design, and is represented in many private collections. Among his commissions are the 20-foot fountain "Science for the World's Well-being," at the Medical Research Laboratories, Groton, Connecticut; The Max Jakob Memorial Award medal of the American Society of Mechanical Engineers; and miniatures in gold, silver, and bronze.

DONALD POLLARD, designer, joined the design staff of Steuben Glass in 1950. A graduate of the Rhode Island School of Design, he had first worked in silver under the trainee program of the Institute of Contemporary Art in Boston, and later tried his hand at architectural theater design. His designs in crystal have been shown in many Steuben exhibitions, including those at Park Lane House, London; the National Gallery of Art, Washington, D.C.; the Metropolitan Museum of Art, New York; and Palais de l'UNESCO, Paris. They are represented also in public and private collections in the United States, Europe, and Asia.

ALEXANDER SEIDEL, painter, was born in Germany. He studied art first in Munich and then, for five years, in Rome. His early work included murals for an industrial concern in Ruedersdorf and settings and costumes for the theater in Berlin. He came to the United States in 1939. From 1943 to 1961 he was staff artist for the American Museum of Natural History, New York, where he illustrated many ornithological books and scientific papers and painted murals of extinct birds, saurians, and primates. He has provided illustrations for *Collier's Encyclopedia* and the *Encyclopedia Americana* and has published two books for young people, about wild birds and water mammals.

ELIZABETH SILVAGNI, painter, teaches art at Cardinal Cushing College, Brookline, Massachusetts. She studied in Boston at the School of the Museum of Fine Arts with Karl Zerbe and at the Boston Museum Summer School with Oskar Kokoschka. She received a B.S. degree in art education from Tufts University and an M.F.A. degree from Boston University. In 1952 a Ruth Sturdevant Scholarship gave her thirteen months of study in Italy and France. Among her works are paintings in public and private collections and the Stations of the Cross for St. Jerome's Nuns Chapel, South Weymouth, and for the Librairie St. Michel, Boston.

GEORGE THOMPSON, senior staff designer for Steuben Glass, joined the company's design department upon its formation in 1936. Born in Nebraska, he received a B.S. in architecture from the University of Minnesota and an M.S. in architecture from Massachusetts Institute of Technology. He was awarded the M.I.T. Class Medal and the Boston Institute of Architects Prize for 1936. His designs in crystal have been included in every Steuben Glass exhibition held since 1937. They are represented in the permanent collections of many museums including, among others, the Metropolitan Museum of Art, New York; William Rockhill Nelson Gallery, Kansas City; Palais du Louvre, Paris; and the National Gallery of Modern Art, New Delhi.

ROBERT VICKREY, painter, studied at Yale University, where he received B.A. and B.F.A. degrees, at the Art Students League, and with Kenneth Hayes Miller and Reginald Marsh. His paintings are in private collections in this country and abroad and in the permanent collections of many museums, including, among others, the Whitney Museum, Atlanta Art Association, Museu de Arte Moderna in Rio de Janeiro, and Dallas Museum of Fine Arts. Among his awards have been the Edwin Austin Abbey Mural Fellowship and Prize, the S. J. Wallace Truman Prize at the National Academy of Design, and

first prize at Florida Southern College International Art Exhibition.

TOM VINCENT, painter, received his first scholarship at the age of six to study at the Nelson Gallery of Art in Kansas City, Missouri. With subsequent scholarships he studied at the University of Kansas City and the Kansas City Art Institute, obtaining an M.F.A. degree. He danced the ballet professionally, played semiprofessional football, and created stage settings in New York before deciding to devote his time to painting and teaching. Among his awards for painting have been first and second prizes at New Jersey State Shows and the Speiser Memorial Prize from the Pennsylvania Academy of the Fine Arts in 1962.

SIDNEY WAUGH, sculptor and chief associate designer for Steuben Glass since 1933, has received many awards, including the Prix de Rome and the Herbert Adams Memorial Award for outstanding contribution to American sculpture. Son of a college professor, he was born in Amherst, Massachusetts, and studied at Amherst College, Massachusetts Institute of Technology School of Architecture, and the École des Beaux Arts in Paris. He was a pupil and assistant of Henri Bouchard. His works include sculptures for the United States Federal Courts Building, Washington, D.C.; Johns Hopkins University; and the United States Battle Monument in Florence, Italy. His designs in crystal are represented in museums and private collections throughout the world.

DON WIER, designer, painter, and graphic artist, joined the design staff of Steuben Glass in 1945. A graduate of the University of Michigan, he studied art at the Chicago Academy of Fine Arts and at the Grand Central School of Art, New York. There he became a member of the faculty and taught for eight years. His early work included portraits of children, flower paintings, and book illustrations. His designs in crystal appear in many private and public collections, including those of the Detroit Institute of Arts, the Musées Royaux d'Art et d'Histoire in Brussels, and Lincoln Center for the Performing Arts, New York.

Steuben Glass FIFTH AVENUE AT FIFTY-SIXTH STREET
NEW YORK 22, NEW YORK